Also written by Foluso Gbadamosi

Dream on, Dreamer

Unleash Your SuperPowers

Unleash YOUR SUPERPOWERS

Discover the power of your talents

Foluso Gbadamosi

National Library of Nigeria Cataloguing-In-Publication Data

GBADAMOSI, Foluso.

Unleash Your Superpowers/ Foluso Gbadamosi, - Cgnature Creativemedia, Shangisha, Lagos , Nigeria.

1. Self actualization (Psychology)
2. Success (Psychology)

I Title

BV 4598.2.G128 2022

ISBN: 978-978-794-188-1 AACR2

Published by
Cgnature Creativemedia Ltd.
19, Mabinuori Street, Off Association Road
Sangisha, Near Magodo Ph 2, Lagos.
t: +234.708.684.2032
e: cgnaturestudio@gmail.com

For information on distribution, translation, or bulk sales, please contact:
Foluso Gbadamosi
Email: me@folusogbadamosi.com

Cover, Layout & Print
Cgnature Creativemedia // +234 (0) 708 684 2032

Cover Image by TY Bello

Printed in Nigeria

Dedication

FOR THE SUPERHUMAN in every one of us waiting to be revealed. Your time has come. It's time to embrace your SuperPowers – those unique strengths, abilities, talents and giftings you possess.

It's showtime!

Acknowledgement

I HAVE ALWAYS been intrigued by our differences as people and how – when understood, honoured, and valued – those differences make the world a much better place. My far-from-scientific research on successful people over the years has revealed one finding: successful people discover, develop, and deploy their uniqueness with dogged intentionality. In other words, they identify their unique talents and innate giftings, accidentally or intentionally, and wield it to their advantage in business, career, ministry, relationships, etc.

Before labelling them as SuperPowers with the help of useful and life-changing assessments, such as the ***CliftonStrengths***® Assessment and the Myers-Briggs Type Indicator® (MBTI®), my idiosyncrasies were a source of frustration to me and well-meaning people in my life. I questioned several aspects of my personality till I realized they were, in fact, SuperPowers. This was easily the most liberating discovery of my 30s. I felt so liberated that it became one of my life's missions to liberate others. I proceeded to become a ***Gallup***® Certified Strengths Coach with a sole desire to help other people discover their own talents – their SuperPowers – and in applying them daily, reach their full potential.

To my parents – my dear late father, Mr. Remi Olowude OON, and my amazing mother, Mrs. Bunmi Olowude—who never stopped telling me there was something extra special about me even when I did not believe there was, I am incredibly grateful.

To my nearest and dearest, my special and unique husband and daughters – Olaleye, Simisola and Tumininu – and my wonderful siblings – Sade, Bukky and Andrew.

To the amazing team of people who pushed me to achieve this - Simisola, Timoni, Molade and Eniola to name a few, I am extremely grateful and you guys are the best.

In you all, I constantly see the beauty and impact of different SuperPowers. Thank you all for everything, I love and appreciate you very much.

Contents

Author's Note

ABOUT TEN YEARS ago, I got really restless. I couldn't articulate the restlessness because I simply did not understand it. I just wasn't comfortable with where I was, which was baffling because I wasn't doing too badly in life.

Going by the definition of success for a woman who just began her 30s where I'm from, I had it good. I had two degrees, had a job, was married, had popped a baby, all that good stuff. Check, check, check! However, deep down inside, I was restless. There was a very deep sense of dissatisfaction, of feeling like I was not where I was supposed to be – whatever that meant, because I had no idea where I was supposed to be. I knew I wasn't entirely happy with my job at the time. I felt there was more to life than the daily grind – wake up, go to work, work (or attempt/ pretend to), leave work, sleep, rinse, and repeat. At the time, I was convinced my purpose was largely tied to my career so discontentment with my job metamorphosed into generalized discontentment. I was convinced that once I "fixed" my professional life by finding a new job in line with my "purpose", all will be well. This thrust me on to the long-winded path of soul-searching lined by variations of those existential questions you may be all too familiar with: 'Why did God create me?', 'What talents do I have?', 'What is my purpose?', 'What difference was I created to make?' I would ponder and ponder and ponder.

I am a pretty logical person and given my birth position as firstborn in my family, a natural problem solver. So, faced with this challenge of discontentment in my career and a barrage of unanswered questions about my purpose and calling, I went on a hunt for resources and assessments that could point me in the right direction. I took just about every online diagnostic test I could lay my hands on. From the ***Myers Briggs***® Test to the Four Temperaments test, you name it. Once I found a test or assessment, I would take it, download the results, print them out and digest every word voraciously. I also hounded different people around me (my husband, my friends, my family members, colleagues) with questions such as: "What do you think I'm naturally good at?", "What do you think my gifts and talents are?", "What are my strengths?" As far as I was concerned, I did not have any unique gifts or talents to map a purpose-driven career around. In my head, I was gift-less and talentless, just a regular person. To me, talents and gifts were the things the Oscars, the Emmys, the Nobel Prizes, and all other award-distributing platforms were about. I was far from receiving any of those awards so, clearly, I was neither talented nor gifted. It didn't help that I was surrounded by people who seemed to have obvious, God-given, innate abilities that shaped their career paths and I did not! I was really in my own head. It felt like everything was working against me.

After one too many tests and assessments, trees massacred from printing out the results, and gruelling interviews grilling people around me about their perceptions of me, I did start feeling a bit more settled as I gained a deeper awareness of self, my strengths, weaknesses, personality, values and more. However, I was still convinced that I had to shape my career around my "purpose" and was unrelenting in my search for an idyllic "purpose-driven career path". I still believed that my purpose, and the fulfilment operating within it promised, was largely linked to my career.

Fast forward a few years, I had an epiphany which could only have been divinely inspired. I came to the realization that I had been living a lie. Unlike what many of us have been taught, purpose is not tied to a career, marital status, parental status or any such compartment of life. Though crucial to our existence on earth, the compartments of our lives are not the only reason God created us! God created each of us with unique talents, which He expects us to discover, develop and deploy in all areas of our lives. This is so we can achieve our ultimate purpose as humans: to dominate. Essentially, no single area of our lives has a monopoly over purpose. Applying our identified God-given talents, no matter how seemingly mundane, in our daily lives is a sure path to achieving purpose. Ultimately, we are all here to make the world a better place in our own way, with our talents, no matter how inconsequential they may seem to us! This epiphany was life-changing for me and released me from the arduous chase after my "dream job" to now living my dream life – a purpose-driven life – today.

In 2019, I randomly discovered the ***CliftonStrengths***® Assessment, followed my instinct and completed it. I had no idea how life-changing it would be for me. While reading the results, I could not believe an assessment could be so precise in capturing my thoughts, feelings and behaviours in a way that brought me to an overwhelming awareness of my strengths and capabilities. I realized that embedded in my natural makeup were raw talents, which when developed, become the very strengths that allow me to live a life of purpose. This simple formula applies to individuals as it does to organizations.

As you read this book, my hope is that you kickstart or continue the journey of discovering your talents, proceed to deploying them in different areas of your life, develop them into strengths, and ultimately dominate your world by living a life of purpose. Here are the steps in a nutshell:

- Discover (Seek).
- Deploy (Intentional Use).
- Develop (Training).
- Dominate (Mastery).

CHAPTER ONE

You Have SuperPowers!

"

Our talents represent our capacity to do things.

"We all have genius within us, never doubt that fact."

— Catherine Pulsifer

BEFORE RISING TO the pinnacle of fame and success, Oprah Winfrey worked in local media during her high school senior year. She was both the youngest female news anchor and the first black female news anchor at her local radio station. She was so good at reciting the late-night news on camera that she soon received a $40,000 salary offer from a television station in Atlanta, a big feat for a 19-year-old in 1973.

Although her career appeared to be on track, she was once 'demoted' from being a news anchor to a writing and reporting role, declared 'unfit for TV' because she could not separate her emotions from the predicaments of those on the news she covered. She even once notably donated her blankets and supplies to a family who had lost their belongings in a fire incident she covered. Though declared "unfit for

TV," Oprah came to recognize her true talents when she took up a job co-hosting a show, she realized just how much she simply enjoyed "chatting" during the show with an ice-cream vendor.

The show was renamed "The Oprah Winfrey Show" by pushing yet another third-rate local Chicago talk show to first place by focusing on current and controversial issues rather than traditional women's issues, and it dominated the airwaves for 25 years. Many guests on Oprah's talk show found themselves revealing personal matters they would not have imagined telling anyone, let alone on television, thanks to Oprah's powerful ability to connect, empathize and communicate with people. She would often cry as people shared their sad stories, ranging from the loss of a pet to discrimination and abuse. Her straightforward curiosity and sense of humour also brought many geopolitical and social issues to the forefront, giving them a global audience. According to a news article written by Les Payne, she is "wittier, more genuine, and far better attuned to her audience" than any other top talk-show host.

Due to the narrow definition given to talents, strengths, core abilities, and other areas of dominance over the centuries, most people have limited the definition of talents to overt abilities like painting, drawing, writing, dancing, acting, athletics, music, and the likes. Not many people realize that much of what we enjoy doing and excel at stems from our innate configuration; a combination of traits that helps us approach issues and solve problems differently from others around us, bringing our own SuperPowers to the table. This is the key message of this book: shifting our focus away from the more popular definitions of talent to the 'imperceptible' uniqueness of our makeup that informs what we enjoy, excel or struggle at, and why.

Talents. Strengths. Skills. Knowledge.

Throughout this book, these terms would be used to describe the road to discovering and harnessing our SuperPowers, which is why understanding what each refers to in clear terms is key to the whole process.

- **Talents:** Your innate abilities.
- **Strengths:** The exceptional and extraordinary results of your talents when they have been intentionally developed.
- **Skills:** A learned ability; it does not have to be innate.

- **Knowledge:** facts, information, and skills acquired through experience or education; the theoretical or practical understanding of a subject (Oxford Dictionary, n.d.).
- **SuperPowers:** Your Strengths.

The ***CliftonStrengths®*** approach, which is a fundamental part of this book, was developed after three decades of studying top achievers in different fields. The approach curated more than 400 themes of talents, out of which about 34 were prevalent. The ***CliftonStrengths®*** assessment assesses your top domains of talent where you effortlessly lead, placing your top five at the apex of the pyramid and the least in comparison at the bottom of the pyramid. This is not to say that you don't possess any of the others on the list, the assessment simply focuses on your area of talents and strengths to aid you in maximizing them.

Gallup® defines talents as repeated patterns, thoughts, and behavioural tendencies that create positive and valuable results when productively applied. Talents are natural, very specific, and are deployed in the uniqueness of how we handle things. Everyone has talents and they energize us naturally. They are such unique, naturally occurring abilities within us that ***Gallup®*** research has shown that only 1 in 33 million people have the same order of talents as you do in the ***CliftonStrengths***® assessment. You are that unique, your SuperPowers are special.

Your Talents ENERGIZE you naturally.

Our talents represent our capacity to do things. For us, they are automatic and are as naturally occurring to us as breathing. This is one of the reasons we may not recognize them as talents because we are used to deploying them with ease. Most of us believe that our talents must be extraordinary, and because they come so easily to us, we fail to recognize how much better we are at these things than many people around us, limiting our inherent connection to our SuperPowers and our ability to maximize them.

There is a connection between your ***talents*** and your ***achievements***. Although the interplay between your talents varies based on each activity you carry out, each talent can help you excel in multiple areas of achievement. For emphasis, each time you carry out an activity seamlessly, you should be sure that one of your talents was involved in making that activity just about effortless for you. For instance, Oprah Winfrey's ability to empathize, connect with guests, and create an atmosphere conducive for them to openly share on her talk show was a distinctive factor that made her show an exceptional success!

The ***Gallup***® approach measures talents such as your ability to take a more critical approach to what others might easily accept as truth (analytical); your ability to draw strength from introspection and high mental activity (intellection); your ability to see potential in others sometimes before they do (maximizer); your love for seeking a common ground during conflicts (harmony); and 30 other talent themes reflected in the way you do things rather than what you do. Our talents are rarely hidden, they are seen in the things that come more easily to us than others. For Oprah Winfrey, it was 'figuring out that she was better at chatting with people than covering news about murder and mayhem'.

According to ***Gallup***®, a ***strength*** is the ability to consistently provide near-perfect performance in a specific activity. Talents are like "diamonds in the rough" – just like diamonds in the earth, we all have naturally-occurring domains of talents that stand us out from others in our approach to matters. In the same way diamonds only become highly sought-after stones when cut and polished, your talents go through the process of honing and growth that builds them into a strength. We will use the terms 'talents' and 'strengths' interchangeably since talents are the raw materials while strengths are the developing/ developed products of talents.

The distance between turning your talents into strengths is covered by what you do to intentionally develop them.

Talent (a natural way of thinking, feeling, or behaving)

X

Investment (time spent practicing, developing your skills, and building your knowledge base)

= **Strength** (the ability to consistently provide near-perfect performance)

Image credit: Tom Rath (Strength Finder 2.0)

Skills are the basic ability to perform the specific steps in an activity. What does a skill look like? Adding and subtracting; using software to prepare a report; welding; hewing down a tree; preparing a lesson plan; cutting up ingredients for a meal; and so on. ***Knowledge***, on the other hand, consists of facts and lessons learned. Simply put, knowledge is what you know, and is acquired through education or training and experience. It may be factual knowledge, like the words of a foreign language, the books of the Bible, software features, or the table of periodic elements. It may also be experiential knowledge, which isn't taught in classrooms or in manuals. Experiential knowledge includes the insights or awareness you have gained through direct experience. So, how does having knowledge work? Your knowledge could guide you on how to deal with an upset customer, how to cope with job-related stress, what part of a lesson your students find most difficult or the fastest route to the grocery store.

The combination of skills and knowledge is developed through experience and learning phases like University, serving in a leadership position, public speaking activities, internships and volunteering, etc. While developing your strengths into near-perfect performance may take some time, the process does begin with recognizing what you do differently and nearly effortlessly, as well as what you excel at, what energizes you and gives you some level of fulfilment while you are at it. Therein lie your SuperPowers, and discovering them is just the beginning of the journey.

What your SuperPowers are not.

The self-awareness process that helps us recognize what our SuperPowers are also gives us insight into what they are not! While it may take being in some situations to recognize how much some things go against the very grain of our beings, sifting out what our SuperPowers are not can narrow down our focus to what they are.

The process of recognizing your SuperPowers can begin by first specifying the things you dread doing, the ones that make you anxious and drain you of all energy. If conflict and chaos drain your energy, it may be a pointer to how much you love harmony and how essential order is in helping you thrive.

At three, Oprah Winfrey had been nicknamed "The Preacher" for her ability to recite Bible verses from her memory with ease. She also mock-interviewed her dolls and the crows on the fence. If Oprah had been a computer scientist writing code for hours on end, barely having any interaction with people, she would likely have been very frustrated! Meanwhile, this is a role other people with talents that differ from hers would thrive at.

Some questions you can ask yourself to identify what your potential SuperPowers are not and narrow your talents down are:

- What tasks rarely get easier no matter how many times you have done them?
- What tasks provoke anxiety in you?
- What tasks make you feel inadequate?
- What tasks do you put off until they're unavoidable?

Focus on your SuperPowers.

Studies have shown that we tend to focus more on our areas of weakness than our areas of strength. Even though the intention may be to improve oneself, focusing more on weak points tends to redirect your focus to what you can't do well rather than what you excel at. This typically causes people to undermine their potential as it leads to spending our entire lives chasing what we think we can do better without ever realizing that there are other areas where our genius truly lies. This ultimately helps us become more self-aware, comfortable with acknowledging our weaknesses and intentional in how we manage them to live a more successful life.

A ***Gallup***® study in 2015 revealed that people who use their strengths daily were three times more likely to report having an excellent quality of life. A close study of many people whose names are synonymous with a particular industry today – Nelson Mandela, Tyler Perry, Steve Harvey, Beyonce, Steve Jobs, Bill Gates, John Maxwell, Oprah Winfrey – would reveal a more consistent application of the areas they have perceived to be their strengths instead of focusing on their weaknesses. Knowing and developing your areas of uniqueness lines your quest for your SuperPowers. You spend your years deploying your energy into the areas where you are more likely to excel, which in turn brings you more fulfilment and success.

Another interesting aspect of strengths and why they go beyond your ability to sing or dance is that the discovery of your strengths will help you make more quality decisions regarding your career, business, and by extension, the relationships you allow in your life. This discovery has informed the lives of some of the most successful men and women you could think of in every industry. Oprah Winfrey's ability to connect with people on a deeper level distinguished her TV show from others, cementing her reputation as the Queen of Daytime Television. Nelson Mandela and Mahatma Gandhi are two of history's greatest political influencers and negotiators. Their ability to seamlessly rally people for a cause and find common ground amongst opposing parties effectively put an end to many current socio-political issues affecting their people at the time.

The beauty of approaching your dealings based on your talents is that you have a new approach for managing your weaknesses. Did you find out that you ideate more than you execute? Then you need to work more with people who have strengths in executing. You recognized that you struggle at making friends and initiating conversations, yet you excel at strategic thinking? Then get yourself a partner who excels at conversations and 'wooing' to handle the opener and clinch the deal at your next investors' meeting. A symbiotic relationship with someone who complements your talents, whether in business, career, study or other affairs, begins with recognizing your own talents and leveraging them.

In summary, you and I would both agree without any objection that to "know thyself" is the beginning of all great accomplishments. Your strengths lie way beyond the most common and obvious talents you are familiar with, they lie in how you do everything. They are apparent in the way you think, your approach to your everyday grind, the moments that energize you, the things you handle seamlessly, and the situations that fuel you and make you feel fulfilled. Recognizing these patterns and acknowledging them as a Superpower would help you leverage opportunities and optimize them.

Reflection Questions

1. What do you yearn to do and look forward to doing?

2. What have you accomplished in your life that you are proud of?

3. What skills and activities have accounted for your greatest successes till date?

4. What parts of your job do you do better than other parts or other people?

5. What are your gifts (unique skills and talents) that if fully developed and completely contributed would make a significant impact in your life, community, and world?

6. How best might you use these skills to serve others?

7. What personality factors account for your greatest successes in life so far?

8. What wouldn't be like it is right now if you had not been a part of it? (E.g., a work or volunteer effort. What did you do and what strengths did you use to make that happen?).

CHAPTER TWO

Connecting Your SuperPowers to Your Purpose

"

Purpose is at the crossroads of your talents and passion.

"When you use your passion and your strengths to improve the lives of other people – to serve, to contribute, to impact – that is when it becomes a purpose."

— Jay Shetty.

FROM THE VERY young to the very old, men to women – from the wealthy to the not-so-wealthy, there is such a wild hunt for purpose, our "why", and a fascination with how to get there. In the introduction to this book, I shared my journey to discovering myself and my purpose. On that journey of discovery, the following questions were at the centre of my quest for answers:

- What are my talents and unique giftings?
- What do I do seamlessly without much effort?
- What do I do that brings me great joy?
- Why do I have them?
- How do I apply them?

I was able to navigate the journey of purpose and its connection to my SuperPowers to where I am today, through a series of psychometric assessments, and consistently bombarding my friends and family with questions, being inspired by sermons, divine guidance, and serving others. Now, let's start by understanding the concept of purpose, and the various curves that will accompany our path to purpose discovery.

Purpose, the journey.

When we were born, we were pre-loaded with innate abilities, i.e. talents; these ultimately point us in the direction of our purpose. There is a direct correlation between discovering your talents, developing them into strengths, and discovering your purpose. The late Myles Munroe often said, "When purpose is not known, abuse is inevitable." Purpose is the crux of existence. It's why you are here, and it's at the crossroads of your talents and passion. We are uniquely gifted for a reason, and it is never accidental.

For some, discovering purpose and engaging their unique gifts is revealed through a life-changing experience that leaves a deep impression on them, eventually 'charging' them with the duty of enlightening others in the same field or passing the baton. Consider Tony Robbins, best-selling author of 'Awaken the Giant Within' and 'Money: Master The Game,' for example. Tony grew up with a depressed and abusive mother who remarried several times. As a 12-year-old in a food-insecure household, Tony didn't expect to sit down to Thanksgiving dinner that year – until he heard a knock on their door and saw a stranger standing on their doorstep with a basket of food for their family. That singular event had such an impact on him that it led to the birthing of an initiative to feed millions of people across the USA. For example, in 2014, he collaborated with the Feeding America Foundation to launch the 100 million meal challenge. This is an example of how one's personal experience can unlock a passionate drive for creating positive change and impact in the lives of other people.

The road to discovering and fulfilling purpose is the horizon beyond attaining personal happiness. Contrary to popular belief, our lives and talents do not just revolve around meeting our needs and keeping us happy. The impact we have on the lives of others, the paths we open up for them by honing our talents, and laying a foundation for future generations are all part of our purpose.

Purpose is progressive, a journey of true discovery. For many others, finding purpose can entail navigating life's many twists and turns. Reflection helps them notice a pattern, a reason why they went through each circumstance, allowing them to draw a sense of purpose from their experiences. It is critical to remember that life is a marathon, not a sprint. Navigating life's topography and corners, akin to cross-country racing, can teach us a thing or two about our talents and their applications. For instance, I didn't stop working, nor did I go on a solitary retreat to reflect on my life and find my purpose. I truly believe that purpose is found in motion, in the daily discovery of the things that energize or drain, fulfil or otherwise. Since we do not have the seeming luxury of leaving it all behind to find purpose, instead of feeling stuck and discontent about your current situation, you need to define your 'Why'.

You can begin to do this by asking yourself more questions as to the reasons you do the things you do.

For instance,

- why are you studying this course?
- why are you working in this role?

- why are you a part of this organization?
- why do you have these relationships?
- Why do you love, hate or otherwise your role?
- why do you get involved in the things you get involved in?
- why are you drawn to certain situations, circumstances or people?

The questions are endless.

It's fine if you find that finances are your motivation. However, one of the things reflecting will do for you, beyond forcing you to explore why you do the things you do, is to give you new levels of clarity and also lead you to understand yourself better. You end up navigating life, knowing why you're persisting in a pursuit, possibly finding avenues to express your talents while at it. Reflection can also assist you in redirecting your energy toward more fulfilling endeavours that meet your financial needs while also allowing you to hone your talents.

Having a strong sense of purpose usually drives our goals and influences the decisions we make in life. It has an impact on our relationships, the opportunities we take advantage of, and our overall outlook on life. Many people attach meaning to their careers, appearing successful by societal standards, but are unable to pinpoint the source of their dissatisfaction with their accomplishments. Take a look below to see how high the statistics are.

- One-fourth of employees view their jobs as the number one stressor in their lives.
- Seven out of ten people are neither motivated nor competent to perform the basics of their job.
- Forty-three percent of employees feel anger toward their employers very often as a result of feeling overworked.

The truth is, when you have clarity about your talents, you can function at your best. You feel more confident about your approach to work and how you interact with others. You use less force, you are more authentic, and you operate in your "sweet spot!"[1]

It can be seen as the intersection of your talents, your passion and what pays you. For instance, as seen in

---

1. The Oxford Dictionary defines Sweet Spot as an optimum point or combination of factors or qualities while the Cambridge Dictionary defines it as the particular situation, quality, combination of things, etc. that is the best or most effective possible.

the example of Oprah earlier, she found her Sweet Spot when she discovered the types of reporting she enjoyed the most. She was not just a news reporter, she enjoyed a certain type of reporting and was her best in that zone!

Your purpose is...not tied to a certain type of job.

While many definitions of living a successful and purposeful life are usually tied to excellence in career and high career pursuits, these definitions are inaccurate. The beauty of our talents is their limitless applications to different spheres of life. Your ability to sense other people's emotions can be used to counsel people from various walks of life, work in a trauma ward, write the most relatable script or song lyrics, or, like Oprah, create one of the most engaging TV shows on the planet. This is the beauty of recognizing your raw potential or talent; there is no limit to the ***'how'*** of your application, implying that you can apply your talents in different areas of your life. Whenever you perform a task flawlessly, there's a good chance that one or more of your talents are at work.

As a result, leaving a dissatisfying job or an overbearing employer may not be the first step toward discovering purpose; rather, observing what aspects of your job you enjoy should be your first clue. While I worked as a computer scientist testing code, I lived for the breaks at work and weekends when I could interact more with people. From my interactions with people, I felt refreshed and refueled. In contrast, I always dreaded the resumption of work. That was my first hint: I draw energy from relating with people rather than being all by myself. Working alone for long periods of time drains me immensely.

Not less powerful than someone else's.

One of the self-limiting beliefs that constrains us from maximizing our talents to fulfil purpose is the belief that the talents of others, and by extension, their purpose, is more powerful than ours. We are quick to notice what makes other people stand out. We admire how effortlessly they focus for hours on end to achieve their goals. We admire their seemingly effortless ability to strike up a conversation with a stranger or their ability to come up with ideas on the spot every time... and we also aspire to be like them.

Our thoughts have a way of shaping our life path. I'm a very positive-minded person, I have been so since the day I was born, I naturally see a glass as half-full than half-empty. I recall certain negative comments made by people close to me when I was younger. They made me feel as if there was something wrong with me for always being "happy-go-lucky" and joyful, even when there was no obvious cause to be. I didn't realize it was a talent until I read my ***CliftonStrengths®*** Assessment Report. As I have gotten older and more intentional on my odyssey to self-discovery, I have connected with the Superpower of my Positivity, and it manifests itself in different ways and in different situations. I am the person who will likely bring contagious enthusiasm to the scene. I very naturally encourage others and can help them see what's going well for them regardless of the situation. My report had a statement that struck me so deeply, I decided to embrace this as a true talent —

'Driven by your talents, you may be a bit happier with your own life when you can convince certain individuals they are valuable. Perhaps you express appreciation

for their upbeat attitudes or their special talents.'

The above statement is why I have devoted so much of my time, energy, and resources to helping others discover their talents. I deeply desire for everyone to know they are ***valuable***.

Uniqueness is attractive because it brings variety to the table. Rather than compete, we begin to seek to complement each other. Think of this as the function of the many different parts of our bodies. Our eyes, ears, nose, and feet all serve different purposes and complement each other in their service to the body. Suppose the nose thinks that the ability to see is more important than supplying the body with oxygen; how would the body survive being oxygen-deprived? Or what if our feet believe they should be the mouth because they get to 'taste the good things in life' instead of hitting the ground? How will we move?

We all serve different purposes. Our unique combination of talents is given to serve ***specific*** purposes, which is why only 1 in 33 million people has the same set of talents as you do in a ***CliftonStrengths®*** Assessment. More precisely, when your ***CliftonStrengths®*** Assessment shows that you share a talent with someone you know, you will find that your Insight reports are not the same. This is because, in the same way, the nose and mouth are very connected and can sometimes serve the purpose of the other in the event of nasal congestion, their customary purpose still makes each body part distinct from the other. Recognize and value your individuality. You are no less special than anyone!

Purpose and Talent: the intersection.

Our strengths and talents are not given to us for ourselves alone. Though they serve us in different ways, they can also serve others. Like everyone else, you've been blessed by God with a deep reservoir of untapped potential. That potential is your talent, waiting to be discovered and put to use in your life. When your talents are connected to your purpose, you have not only found a way to build your talents into strengths, you have also unlocked the door to a more satisfying and impactful life. A ***Gallup***® research reveals that people who use their strengths every day are:

- 3x more likely to report having an excellent quality of life.
- 6x times more likely to be engaged at work.

- 8% more productive.
- 15% less likely to quit their jobs.

When you discover your talents and begin to add the knowledge and skills required to develop them into strengths, you will discover new ways to serve and do more to improve, not only your own life but the lives of others. One of the core characteristics of purpose is impact, i.e. or the difference we can make in the lives of others. There are many unforgettable people in history who left indelible marks in the sands of time due to how they deployed their unique strengths for others.

Mother Teresa, who dedicated her life to humanitarian efforts to save the lives of the poorest of the poor, used her talents, exposure, background, and resources to transform lives in her community and all over the world. In the same vein, honing our talents into strengths includes a blend of our exposure, training, and background. This uniqueness can serve to redefine the lives of people.

A ready example of areas to apply your strengths in fulfilling your purpose is the United Nations' Sustainable Development Goals (SDGs). By recognizing your authentic self and abilities, your talents can intersect with purpose as you make a ***transformational*** rather than ***transactional*** impact in the lives of people. The impact does not have to start out huge. Begin by proposing solutions to the problems in your immediate environment.

In the end…

We rarely consider the end of our lives. The end of life usually feels so far away that we often don't think about it as much as we think about our purpose.

Choosing how you want to be remembered at the end of your life allows you to live in accordance with your purpose. Nobody wants to spend their final days in regret. Knowing that you had the ability to make certain changes, enjoy certain roles and relationships more, use your SuperPowers to transform the lives of others but didn't, can make anyone miserable. Connecting your SuperPowers to your purpose ultimately means that you can face the end of your life without regret, knowing that no resource (talent) given to you went unused.

The wonder of talents is how they define everything we do. So, stop worrying about how much your current situation limits your ability to use your SuperPowers. If you feel that way, kindly re-evaluate your position and find ways to incorporate your SuperPowers into your situation. Change the lens through which you view your current circumstances, and your experience will change. By implementing your SuperPowers in your current endeavours, you can truly begin the process of transforming your talents into strengths and thus get on the journey towards fulfilling your purpose.

Reflection Questions

1. What are your innate talents?

2. How can you intentionally develop them into strengths?

3. Where, in your life, can you add the greatest value?

4. How will you ultimately measure your life?

CHAPTER THREE

Discovering Your Genius Zone

"

The road to discovering your talents and SuperPowers is a very intentional one.

"Until you make the unconscious conscious, it will direct your life and you will call it fate."

— C.G Jung.

ARIANA JOHNSON'S AWARD and ensuing promotion to the position of Customer Experience Manager didn't come as a shock to anyone, not even the regular visitors to the bank. For the customers, her ability to set them at ease no matter what issue had them frowning deeply on a Monday morning was second to none. Some others remembered that their first contact with her was when they visited the bank to get their debit cards. Not only did she converse briefly with them and make them feel seen while they waited, but she also helped each person set up the bank's app on their phones without ever switching her pleasant expression over never-ending questions. Another customer particularly remembered how she got her daughter, who is unusually anxious, to warm up to her in such a short time. She definitely deserved the third-time award, including the accompanying promotion.

Ariana, on the other hand, was pensive. With her new job description, she would no longer be able to meet people one-on-one, a task she enjoyed immensely. Her new role was more strategic and supervisory. She would rarely speak with clients directly unless they had issues that needed her intervention. She couldn't complain about her pay and all seemed great with her enviable position, but then her major worry was whether she would excel at this role and enjoy it as much as in her previous role. She decided to spend the weekend before resumption highlighting the requirements in her job description and what she could do to excel in her capacity.

As she worked, her fears began to dissipate. One of the other reasons she got promoted was the strategic ideas she shared with her previous team lead, which had increased her unit's revenue generation.

"The strategic goals and policy creation part shouldn't be too difficult then."

Thus began her revelation of sorts about the other "things" she really excelled at, which could come in handy in her new role. Exercising her ability to make strangers feel comfortable may have been her more obvious talent because she used it often in her previous role, but there was more to her than she realized. This should be fun, she thought.

Like Ariana, we sometimes streamline our talents to the more obvious ones and those we are acquainted with. For some, it's enjoying mental activity and a preference for intellectual conversations, or the ability to analyse each course of action which has helped deploy energy more concisely; or even the fascination with the future and seeing possibilities that have brought hope in gloomy situations. When there is a change of state or a new challenge comes our way, it can make us feel out of depth. Oftentimes, because we have only been able to recognize and maximize one or two of our talents, we wonder what we bring to the table in unfamiliar situations.

Some others are like Dave, who didn't discover his talents until he was middle-aged. Dave's father had a government job which required him to be transferred every few years. Unwilling to let the movement affect their bond, Dave's mother insisted that the whole family move with their dad. Due to the constant change, it was difficult for his mother to hold down a job. In between helping the children settle down in new places and being available to them due to their father's constant absence, she was pretty occupied. Then tragedy struck: his father died in an accident while Dave was still in high school. The accident drilled a hole into their family's finances. As the first child, he didn't go to university because funds were unavailable; instead, he worked part-time as a baker to meet the family's needs. Over time, he moved into an entry-level role as a clerk, rising from there to the position of senior manager after 35 years of meritorious government service. Even though the job met his needs and was very secure, a spring of dissatisfaction consistently bubbled within him. He had spent many years working to meet his family's needs, but now that he was retiring, he wasn't sure of the path to explore his own strengths and live a more satisfying life. He was, in fact, convinced that he had no talents until he took the ***CliftonStrengths***® Assessment and discovered what they were.

The road to discovering your talents and SuperPowers is a very intentional one. It usually takes an acknowledgment that there is more to you than meets the eye. A recognition that while you may be as flawed as the other person, you do have some traits that come to you more easily than the other person, the ones that others may have tagged you a weirdo for! If like Ariana you have recognized one or two traits that flow across how you handle everything (for example, you know how to make sense of chaotic situations that may trip others over), you may not necessarily have seen this as a talent – after all, it comes so easily to you so it's not a big deal or you may have also recognized how understated these talents are. There are probably other talents that you have, but they lie partly asleep beneath the layers of your unconscious, springing forth at the most unexpected moments or not because you are yet to fully understand and explore the dimension of possibilities they hold.

Some believe that your desire to find a sense of purpose or understand the dissatisfaction that spirals within you might be a sign of midlife crisis (or an early onset of it because you aren't exactly midlife just yet). However, you realise that you've just somehow lost yourself in the daily motions of making a living. Compromise after compromise has you wondering where your true strengths lie. You've seen the expression of satisfaction on the faces of other colleagues and friends as they take on certain roles. You've seen their modus operandi and you're certain beyond any doubt that this unique extra way of discharging their duties goes beyond the training they have had. They simply have the extra touch that makes them stand out from others in the same role, who underwent the same training as they did...and you want the same thing for yourself.

The journey to discovering your SuperPowers does not have to include a merry-go-round or a 'fumbling in the dark for the light switch' process. A more structured way to discover your SuperPowers would be:

1. Using the strengths approach.

Perspective is everything. For most of us when growing up, our sense of self was forged from a blend of our culture, our upbringing, what people told us about ourselves, what we discovered through our successes and failures, what we discovered through comparing ourselves to others, and more. Many of our cultures constantly remind us of the ways we aren't good enough. Advertisements are rife with how we compare to others who are suave and have their life more put together than reality allows. Although this sells the product, it's a constant reminder of where we supposedly fall short – which is absolutely human. However, this often colours the way we see ourselves. We are more likely to point out where we fall short than to acknowledge the things we excel at. When the light shines on our strengths, we look on with shock, sometimes disbelief! We didn't recognize these as talents or strengths.

To put things more concretely, this is the problem the ***CliftonStrengths®*** Assessment solves. We get too many reminders about how to 'fix ourselves' that we rarely recognize what diamonds we currently hold and need to polish. The strengths approach to our talents does not obliterate our weaknesses; rather, it gives us a new perspective to viewing them, increasing our self-awareness, and teaching us how to manage them. Self-awareness is not only a recognition of strength; it also includes an acceptance of weaknesses. For the purpose of this book, weaknesses mean a lack of talent that potentially gets in the way of your success and negatively affects your performance. Under the ***CliftonStrengths®*** Assessment, the 34 themes represent the different areas in which each person is uniquely gifted. When you get the results of the assessment, your five dominant talents top the list and represent the areas that you naturally excel at, while the talents at the bottom of the list represent your least dominant talents.

The strengths approach teaches you how to manage weaknesses through leveraging the strengths of others and sometimes by managing yourself better. **Instead of focusing so much on our weaknesses or letting them hang over the sunshine of our strengths like a dark cloud, we find ways to manage them.** A strengths-based approach increases your self-acceptance and confidence. Where you would typically see the ways you do not measure up, you begin to see the areas of talent where you flourish and the environments that encourage it. Where you may be afraid to accept new opportunities, you begin to see the possibilities of excelling in them, and the uniqueness you bring to the table that makes the same endeavour stand out. Suddenly, you know why you may have been having some conflict at work, in personal relationships, and more! It opens your eyes to who you really are and how you have been wired.

2. Self-reflection.

Self-reflection is the act of taking out time to think about, evaluate, and give serious thought to your behaviours, thoughts, attitudes, motivation, and desires. Outside the ***CliftonStrengths®*** Assessment, the journey to discovering your SuperPowers can also begin with self-reflection. Of course, reflecting on your uniqueness rather than weakness. Like Ariana, asking yourself some self-reflection questions can help you notice the patterns in what you do and how you do them.

Here are some questions that can point you towards the patterns *(you would find more at the end of this chapter)*:

- What are your main activities outside of work?

- What do you do that leaves you feeling amazing, alert and alive?
- What activities do you do effortlessly?
- When was the last time you lost track of time carrying out an activity? What activity was this?

3. Asking other people.

A teacher and also a mum, once sighed in exasperation to her daughter. On inquiry, the mum exclaimed that she didn't think she had any talents. Her daughter, mildly surprised, responded, "Why mum, no one else has that unflinching faith in our abilities like you do!" The response was, "Oh. I suppose that's a talent." What this teacher didn't know or value was how she always cheered everyone on to achieve their goals, believing in them even when they didn't believe in themselves. Like their neighbour's 2-year-old son who paid close attention while his mum cooked, or the girl at her daughter's school who held the crowd spellbound during her spoken word session. Almost without trying, she could see the possibilities in each person's behaviour. Even when her husband perceived her encouragement as pressure, she really couldn't help it; she saw the small changes and character modification and it delighted her in no small measure! The people around her were aware of how naturally she deployed this talent and how much satisfaction it brought to witness growth. The conversation with her daughter was truly the eye-opener she needed.

In conclusion, discovering your SuperPowers recreates your world, improves your self-esteem, motivates you to take on new challenges, and gives you a hope and a future to look forward to. Remember that discovering your SuperPowers doesn't have to be a blind fumble, not when you can take the strengths approach.

Reflection Questions:

1. What do you like talking about the most?
2. What would you say three of your greatest strengths are?
3. What do people ask you to do often?
4. What are some things that people say you do well? What do they ask you to teach them or help them with?
5. What do you get complimented on the most?
6. What do you like about yourself?
7. What do you yearn to do and look forward to doing?
8. What skills and activities have accounted for the greatest success in your life?
9. What parts of your job do you do better than other parts or other people?

10. What are your gifts (unique talents) that if fully developed would make a significant impact in your life, community, and world?

11. What personality qualities account for your greatest success in life so far?

12. What would have had a different result had you not been a part of it? (Work or volunteer efforts). What did you do and what strengths did you use to make that happen?

CHAPTER FOUR

Deploy and Develop Your SuperPowers

"

Like muscles, the more you develop your talents, the better they help you achieve your purpose.

"He who has a 'why' to live for can bear almost any 'how'."

— Friedrich Nietzsche.

SO FAR, WE have seen that a Strength is born from the ability to consistently provide near-perfect performance in its related talent. We have also established that the journey to discovering your strengths begins by identifying your talents and then acquiring the knowledge and skills necessary to develop them. This means that it is not enough to recognize your SuperPowers, and then leave them to lie dormant or spend all your life talking about what abilities you have without doing anything productive with them.

Our talents are given to us for a purpose: impacting the lives of others and the world around us – which is why application is more important than mere recognition. Although recognition is sometimes the launchpad for application, recognition is only wholesome when it includes the many areas in which talent can be applied, otherwise the purpose of recognition is not achieved. Deploying your talents is the process of intentionally using your talents in ways that allow them eventually evolve into SuperPowers. Like muscles, developing your SuperPowers requires you to exercise them enough so as to understand how naturally they come to you, what environment helps them thrive, and otherwise.

Talents are the foundation of strengths; therefore, your ability to achieve excellence and make the most of your life depends on the extent to which you develop your talents into strengths. Like diamonds, your talents are most valuable after they have gone through the polishing wheels of skills and knowledge to produce a carefully cut and shining brilliance. Attaining brilliance can take time, possibly several years, like all worthwhile ventures do. **As a matter of fact, there's hardly an 'end' in sight where development is concerned. What happens however is that with each development stage, you unlock new levels of your talent, and it takes you farther and farther from where you started from.**

Like muscles, the more you develop your talents, the better they help you achieve your purpose. The time and hard work invested in learning the skills and knowledge necessary for development is typically evident in the refining process. On this premise, we will delve into seven strategies for refining your talents into strengths:

1. Know your talents.

This seems like an obvious first step, especially in light of the previous chapter. However, there is a key difference between being familiar with your talents – possibly from recognizing patterns in the way you handle things or taking the ***CliftonStrengths***® Assessment – and an awareness of how they have served you.

Perception plays a very influential role in the motivation to develop ourselves. Research has proven that many people either do not believe that they have any talent or that they have talents that are minimal in application. When people believe that they have talent of the bare minimum, they try to avoid activities that reveal their perceived lack of it. Procrastination, for instance, is a common example of a game people play to hide such. They delay working on a task until the last moment so that if they don't succeed, they can blame it on the lack of time rather than the lack of talent. Some others misperceive a strong talent as a weakness, and so avoid any achievement-related activity, not because they are not talented in that area, but due to their misperception of their talents.

To raise the level of your 'knowing' by a notch, take out a sheet and write down your five dominant talents (if you have taken the ***CliftonStrengths***® Assessment) or your perceived talents (if you haven't taken the assessment). In front of each talent, write down situations where these talents have served you. Ariana in our previous chapter used her 'WOO' (***CliftonStrengths***® talent) talents to get the bank's customers to feel like they were meeting a friend. Her 'Strategic' talents also served in raising the revenue from her unit. By taking this exercise, you raise your self-awareness and prepare yourself mentally to begin your talent development drive.

2. Value your talents.

Value recognition is depicted in how the subject is received and handled. When an item is valued, the effort to sustain or increase its perceived value is usually evident in its packaging, storage, and what purpose it serves. Owners of valuable items would typically take on the personal responsibility of maintaining the value of the item, lending it out only on rare occasions and when painstaking care is assured. In the same vein, the perceived value of your talents is seen in how you take full responsibility for their development into a strength. Increase your understanding and appreciation of your talents, and their value will rise exponentially.

When you value them, you will invest the time, energy, and other resources necessary to develop your talents into strengths. This, in turn, increases your confidence and sets the pattern for developing them into strengths. Not many people comprehend how valuable their talents are at first. To correct this misperception, think back to some of your proudest moments or a moment when you were doing something you really enjoyed. Highlight what talent(s) you deployed to achieve what you did. Now imagine not having this at all or very little of it. Do you get the picture now?

Your talents are invaluable but your perception of them plays a huge role in determining whether or not they would become strengths and how much time this would take.

3. Talents and the big 'Why'.

Talents are most powerful when inspired by a personal mission. Without an overarching goal or purpose for your life, your talent development plan may fall through the cracks. What do you hope to achieve in life? What do you want to be remembered for? For everything you do, ask yourself why you are doing it.

By connecting your talents to your ***'Why'***, your motivation to invest in developing your talents into strengths is heightened. As a result, your talents being turned into strengths empowers you to actualize your personal mission. Take a moment to pen down your big Why(s) while also highlighting the different ways you think that your talents can help in achieving your mission. Even though strategies can change over a period of time, the destination hardly ever changes, and this plan will serve as the launchpad for a truly meaningful talent development process.

4. Strengthening relationships.

No man is an island. The process of talent development and deployment is therefore incomplete without the right relationships to hold us accountable, respect our goals, and oil our engines when we start to creak. In fact, the American Society of Training and Development (ASTD) found that people are 65% more likely to meet a goal after committing to another person.

What then should characterize the relationships that strengthen our talent development process?

- **Mutual respect:** Neither party should look down on the other.
- **Openness and honesty:** You should be able to have transparent and open conversations with said person(s).
- **Encouragement:** Your accountability relationship should be one that encourages you when you are demotivated or fearful to take on challenging opportunities.
- **Understanding:** The relationship should be characterized by understanding, a willingness to actively comprehend how you both tick, so as to have a mutually beneficial relationship.
- **Good listening:** Your relationship must feature good listening skills, allowing you to properly engage and empathize with the other person.

When your relationship(s) feature these healthy characteristics, you will be able to:

- Work together to create talent development plans that are tailored to each or an intersection of both your talents.
- Check milestones in your talent development process and work together to create new ones.

- Report on your efforts, shortfalls, and experiences in the talent development process.
- Receive honest feedback that will spur you on or curb your excesses.
- Form a relationship that pushes you to greatness and helps you make the most of your life.

5. Practice.

As they say, practice makes perfect. Practice and intentional use of your talents not only strengthens them: you learn and relearn from experience what skills and knowledge you have perfected and what other areas need some more focus.

Practice should also begin where you are, you don't have to wait for what you consider to be the perfect environment or circumstances. Engage and apply your talents at work, in choosing your university courses, in accepting and vying for leadership opportunities, in choosing extracurricular activities to get involved in and more. Draw up a plan that works well with your schedule and current environment, and then work your way up from there. In the words of Tim Ferriss, **"...you succeed because you find your unique strengths and focus on developing habits around them."**

6. Training/Books/Podcasts.

Life-long learning is not a luxury, it's a necessity. Continuous learning is an antidote to being obsolete in the ever-changing world we live in. In a quest to develop and deploy your strengths, expose your mind to information sources that redefine your perception of your talents and equip you with multiple development action plans. Exposing your talents to the light of new information helps you find newer ways to employ your talents even with familiar projects.

However, to prevent being overwhelmed by the many resources that may be available in developing your strengths, create a strategy over the next week or month for optimizing these learning resources and applying them. The best strategies are usually a mix of reading, online video courses, podcasts, and hands-on experience. Push yourself outside your comfort zone and watch growth begin. Then observe and reflect on how much stronger your talents have become over the period. Rinse and repeat.

The talent-based action points in the ***CliftonStrengths***® Assessment results are another launchpad to kickstart your talent development journey. They contain Action Points that help you add value to both your life and those of the people around you. Look through your assessment results and ponder on the action points.

Begin using them from where you are and work your way up from there.

7. Create a vision board.

A vision board is a visual representation of your goals and what you want to accomplish. It's crafted to inspire you to drive forward in attaining your goals. Unlike writing down your plans, crafting a vision board is a quick reminder of where you plan to be and what being there looks like. It can be very powerful in propelling you to bring your plans to fruition.

Psychologists believe that mental practices like visualization increases your motivation and confidence in achieving your dreams. Brought into the context of deploying your SuperPowers, you need to **remember that the different expressions of your talents are meant to fulfil your purpose and not anyone else's.**

To deploy and develop your SuperPowers, craft your vision board of where you see your talents taking you, as far as your mind's eye can see. The vision can be modified as you proceed on the journey, but it is always good to begin with a feasible end in mind.

In conclusion, building talents into strengths involves

a lot of intentionality, much like building physical strength. Deploying and developing our talents improves our self-confidence and helps us make the most out of our lives. **The path to mastery is usually a lot shorter when it is focused on maximizing your strengths rather than focusing on your weaknesses.**

Reflection

1. Draw up a plan that helps you maximize your talents using the resources and platforms available to you currently. Implement your strategy over a period of time, then measure your results and review your blind spots. Rinse and repeat.

2. Get accountability for your talent development process while taking into account the characteristics of a healthy relationship mentioned in this chapter.

3. Become a talent scout! Identify talents in others, celebrate others talents and also build a community that lets you leverage on the talents of others.

4. Create a vision board or an action plan that inspires and motivates you to deploy and develop your talents into strengths.

CHAPTER FIVE

Dominate Your World

"

To dominate your world is to develop your SuperPowers until your voice matters.

"I have things to say and I'll say them."

— Chimamanda Ngozi Adichie.

BORN IN NSUKKA, Enugu State, Nigeria, Chimamanda Ngozi Adichie is famous for her novels, her strong stance on feminism, and TED talks like ***The Danger of a Single Story***. But she didn't rise to the spotlight overnight. She was an early reader who started from the age of 4. At 10, she had read Chinua Achebe's Things Fall Apart, an immense inspiration to her. As a Medicine and Pharmacy student at the University of Nigeria, Nsukka her love for writing led her to edit a magazine run by the university's Catholic medical students. She also spent a lot of time going to the library to research and study how to get published in the days before search engines were the norm. Even though she got good grades, after 2 years of studies, she realised that her SuperPowers were better applied to a course that was not Medicine! She decided to alter her course completely by studying for the SAT's. Fortunately, she received a scholarship to study Communication and Political Science at Drexel University, Philadelphia, before transferring to Eastern Connecticut State University to complete her studies.

In between her editorial role at the University of Nigeria and her first award-winning novel in 2004, Purple Hibiscus, Chimamanda published a collection of poems in 1997 ***(Decisions)*** and a play ***(For Love of Biafra)*** in 1998 amongst other publications. Asides from her other award-winning novels like ***The Thing Around Your Neck*** and ***Half of a Yellow Sun***, her short stories and essays like ***Notes on Grief, Dear Ijeawele,*** and ***Zikora*** have also garnered a lot of media attention. Her siblings used to wonder why she loved to climb up to her father's study to read for hours on a perfectly sunny day. Her ability to take a step back, see a problem from a variety of different angles, and come up with solutions has aided in the development of many controversial characters in her novels and in making her speeches renowned.

Like a truly analytical person, Chimamanda hardly goes with the grain of events just because 'that is the way things are done'. She peels off layer after layer of events to find out the root cause of issues. Even though she extends understanding to people on their stance over matters, for her, the theories and ways of reasoning have to be logical before she can adopt them. This talent is evident in her style of writing and speaking, which sets her apart from other African writers. Undoubtedly, Chimamanda is a natural leader and facilitator of change as her TED talk titled ***The Danger of a Single Story***, which focuses on the power of stories to shape stereotypes, has been adapted as an academic resource across the world.

Dominance is Influence.

Dominance comes from an intersection of your hard work and talents being built into strengths through the acquisition of the required skills and knowledge. The road to dominance is lined with the grit needed to exercise your talents again and again, rise and fall on endeavours, acknowledge the gaps in your knowledge, and submit yourself to filling them.

Dominating your world is what transforms your talents into SuperPowers. Like Chimamanda, like Wole Soyinka, like Oprah, like Steve Jobs, and a host of others whose names have become synonymous with a particular industry/cause because they have applied their talents over and over in that space.. It's worth reiterating that the application of your talents is seen in the 'how' you do things. In that sense, you are limitless in your application – whether as a student, someone in a junior role, as a startup founder, in a leadership role or whatever capacity you occupy. The aim is to grow, to develop your SuperPowers by applying them over and over again until you are well known for what you do nearly effortlessly. Here begins the journey to dominance.

Dominance is also embodied in the societal changes you are able to drive with your voice and your presence. Influence is defined as the capacity to cause a change, to have an effect on someone or something, or to determine an outcome. To dominate your world is to develop your SuperPowers until your voice ***matters***, which can cause a paradigm shift or pull the rug from under stereotypes. Feminism has been redefined following Chimamanda's novels and TED talk titled, 'We should all be feminists.' Michael Jackson's music and voice shed light on world issues, such as climate change, AIDS, and cancer research. Chinua Achebe changed the narrative about how stories about West Africans are told. Oprah's long-standing commitment to protecting children from abuse led to the signing of the 'Oprah Bill' into law in 1993. There are endless examples of people who have been able to turn their talents into SuperPowers, and how they are using that to influence their communities and the world at large. In the same way, our talents are not given to us to serve ourselves alone, but to also create impact. By extension, our endeavour to develop our talents until we dominate in our areas of influence should not be limited to living an excellent quality of life only, but also encompass lending our voices to the areas in need of change...of which there are plenty!

The bottom line is that dominance is an uphill task that demands hard work and intentionality while developing your talent. Dominance leads to ***impact*** and impact brings about ***influence***.

Dominance is Leadership.

Greg McKeown, in his book Effortless, says, "Whenever you want far-reaching impact, teaching others to teach can be a high-leverage strategy." Deploying your talents to a dominance level can begin in leading others by teaching them, by identifying & leveraging their strengths to achieve goals and more. One piece of advice that people often follow blindly is to spend time attempting to develop weaknesses as strengths, when really, we ought to acknowledge our weaknesses and leverage the talents of others where we are weak.

The beauty of the strengths perspective is that we don't just recognize our strengths, we recognize the strengths of others, allowing us to maximize their strengths just as much as we maximize ours.

To dominate by leadership:
Offering to lead gives an opportunity to showcase and develop your strengths while leading others from a strengths perspective.

i. **Lead with your talents while complementing your weaknesses.** There are several academic theories that discuss the various leadership styles and how each has a different effect on a group. The idea is to choose the type of leader you want to be rather than the type of leader you are. Leading from a position of strength allows you to lead your team in the best way, that is, by recognizing everyone's natural talents and positioning them accordingly. **This helps you build high performance teams and makes you great leader!**

In the words of Bob Gass, **"Unless you learn to delegate, you'll disintegrate."**

The ***CliftonStrengths***® Assessment report assesses the various themes through which a person leads:

- **Executing** – These are the DOERS! They know how to make things happen! They can take your ideas, your vision and turn them into reality. They make things practical and know how to implement.

- **Influencing** – These people know how to gather momentum and are comfortable taking charge! They speak up and make sure others are heard. They bring attention to change, can convince others and influence them.
- **Relationship Building** – They can build strong relationships and are often emotionally intelligent. They have people skills and can hold different types of groups together e.g., work teams, families and more.
- **Strategic Thinking** – These are the critical thinkers, the ones who absorb and analyze information that can inform better decisions. They also know how to stretch others thinking as they come up with different ideas.

I have a group of friends and we all lead very differently. I lead with Influencing closely followed by Relationship Building. ***A*** leads with Executing while ***B*** leads with Strategic Thinking also closely followed by Relationship Building.

When we work together, our approach always differs and since we became intentional in discovering and deploying our talents, we see the beauty in our differences and leverage our specific strengths.

All ***A*** needs to hear is the idea and immediately jumps into DOING. She has a to-do list in her head that is ready to go, sometimes to the detriment of others actual talents as she naturally just wants to get things done!

B has endless ideas and always helps us be more creative, due to her strong relationship building talent she also loves for everyone to share their perspectives, sometimes to the detriment of execution.

I immediately start thinking about who needs to know about this project and who else needs to be part of it based off their skills and expertise, sometimes this stretches the to-do list longer than it needs to be.

Realising the 'not so good side' of our strengths helps us intentionally manage them and work together to create great results. These are also referred to as Balconies and Basements which the next chapter will dive into. Balconies are the positive characteristics of our talents/strengths while the Basements are the potential negative characteristics.

Leaders who lead from the theme of Execution push their teams to go higher, reach higher, and challenge themselves. Influencing team leaders are more vocal and ensure that others are heard. Leaders who lead via the theme of Relationship Building do a better job of keeping the team together by recognizing the value that each team member brings to the group. Strategic Thinking leaders are forward-thinking, energized by brainstorming sessions and the possibility of what could be. When leaders recognize their own leadership themes, they can develop a customized leadership style. For example, top CEOs such as Elon Musk may lead from themes such as Execution, whereas Mark Zuckerberg may lead from Strategic Thinking. Leading from your talents comes naturally to you as a leader, energizes you, and brings the most fulfilment! However, talents and strengths are not without flaws, as evidenced by the fallout between Steve Jobs and Steve Wozniak. Relationship Building can be a blind spot for a leader who leads from the Executing theme. To make the best of the team's potential, leaders should not only lead from their strengths, but also acknowledge the blind spots of their strengths, by collaborating with others who lead from other themes (e.g., a leader who leads from Strategic Thinking can collaborate with someone who leads with Relationship Building to create a balance in the work environment).

ii. **Have clear goals and get clarity on your role as a leader.** Whether defined personally or assigned by the organization, have clear goals of what you should achieve at the end of it all. Imagine if a follower asks a leader the purpose of a task and the leader says, "I don't know." That would be absurd. Create clear and concise objectives, and know the strengths of each member of the team to understand how each can work together to achieve the set goals. Define what 'done' looks like to you, and you'll be able to map out the daily steps leading to the end you have in mind.

iii. **According to a *Gallup*® research on What Followers Want From Leaders, the traits most coveted by followers are trust, compassion, hope, and stability.** These traits are innate in leaders who rank high in the Developer talent theme and similar talent themes. For others who rank highly on themes like Achiever, talents like compassion may not flow naturally as you are more task-oriented. Check out which of these traits do not come naturally to you; be intentional as you lead knowing you may have to make an effort in those areas (to the best of your ability); and find a strong complementary partnership to lean on to balance the team out.

iv. **Seek out people to mentor you as much as you need people to benefit from what you are teaching.** Mentorship by someone who has gone ahead of you can significantly improve your personal development while providing insights that level the hurdles you may face on this quest. Observe and reflect on what talents other leaders seem to deploy in having the best interaction with their team members. Observe the most outstanding leaders you know and what makes them outstanding to you. What makes these leaders so effective? What are their greatest talents? In what environment and with what groups of people do their talents seem to shine the most?

Dominating your world is a journey.

Let's look at some Clifton Strengths talents that I come across often and how they sometimes manifest in life situations. As you read through, keep in mind what energizes each of the talents. The Diagram below is based on the Four Domains of Leadership Strengths according to CliftonStrengths® and pertain to the examples that follow.

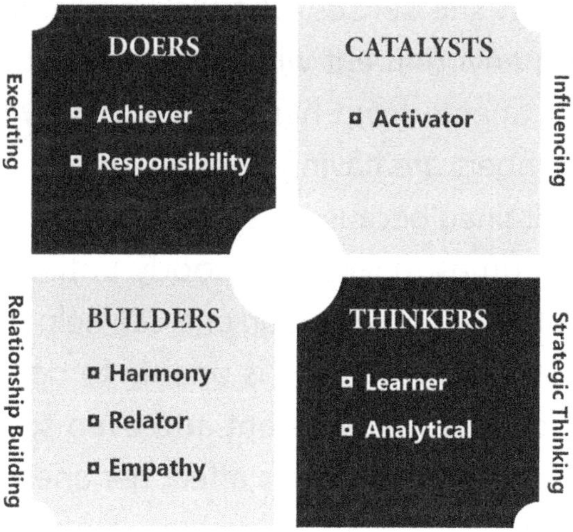

High achiever talents are usually energized and very driven by work, they tend to be tireless and have a high drive to deliver. This can look like being too focused on work with an inability to balance life in a better way. It can sometimes lead to an inability to delegate out of fear of being disappointed by others. Audrey was accused of being a slavedriver and it broke her heart; she couldn't believe it. All she wanted was for the team to deliver on their project and that motivated her daily! In retrospect she realized that she assumed everyone had the same work drive that she did!

Team AKE

Karina leads with ***Relationship Building*** and her top talent is ***Empathy***. She not only senses the feelings of her team members, but she is also usually right about what she senses. She works in a very high achieving environment with people who have very different talents from her. On the days when her team members are having a rough time, she usually ends up drained because she can sense their feelings. This sometimes makes her moody until she has a conversation with the person and can help them feel better. On days when she is unable to do this, she comes across as inconsistent and even sometimes weak because it really does affect her energy in the workplace.

Eric's top talent is ***Responsibility***, and he is fresh out of University with a zeal to take on the world. He takes ownership of what he says he will do and also values honesty a great deal. He lives with his parents and has just started an entry level role working with Karina and Audrey. Eric realizes very quickly that not only does his to-do list seem endless, his work doesn't seem to show the results he should have. While reflecting, he realizes that he has a hard time saying NO and has entirely too many things going on. He gets burnt out very easily and happens to have a discussion with Karina. She advises him to start setting boundaries and using the word 'NO' when he is unable to take on additional commitments especially when they are unrelated to his core role.

After speaking to Eric and picking up on his feelings, Karina spoke to Audrey who really did not understand where she was coming from. As far as Audrey was concerned, Eric had been assigned his responsibilities in a fair way. Karina felt she was not getting through to Audrey and took it as her responsibility to discuss with Ayo, their departmental head. She mentioned that Eric was burnt out and Audrey was a slavedriver who wasn't emotionally intelligent enough to manage the team.

Fortunately, Ayo has several years of experience and picks up on people's talents quite easily. She is able to assess the situation objectively and they have a group meeting to discuss how to better manage their personalities and talents as a team.

Responsibility sometimes looks like commitment to others while it can be burnout to the individual. Managing this talent looks like setting boundaries and intentionally knowing when to say NO.

Andrew is an ***Activator***. He hears an idea and is ready to dive right into execution. He wants to get things done and spend less time talking, more time doing. Andrew hates long meetings without a clear agenda and outcome. Sometimes Andrew comes across as someone who likes to jump into a plan before the actual planning is done. When working with someone who loves to think and plan, it usually causes conflict. However, upon understanding the SuperPower of his Activator talent, Andrew is now more accommodating of others while understanding his own natural patterns of thinking.

Working together and appreciating the talents of others can create a very powerful team.

Ronke leads with ***Relationship Building*** and her top talent is ***Relator***. She thrives on building relationships and working with people she has built them with. She has always worked in family type work cultures which, unknown to her, has really helped her talents develop. Her company has been acquired by a larger organization and she is excited about this until she realizes that the new organization has a very different work culture from what makes her thrive. Her new boss often says the workplace is for results and not for forming friendships. Ronke does not understand this and thinks her boss is quite mean.

Kemi has a top talent in ***Harmony*** and used to work in a very high conflict work environment due to the nature of the job. Her natural talent of seeing both sides of a situation came across as someone who did not like confronting issues and always avoiding conflict. Working with a high achiever boss who had no issue with conflict became a real challenge and it was not until she left this role that she realized how much it had drained her daily.

Lucy is a ***Learner***. She is constantly thinking of how to improve on what she knows, and she loves the process of learning. Her husband Bayo has top talents in the Executing theme and they often clash when things need to get done because Lucy always seems to get lost in what he considers unnecessary. Her husband gets energized by doing, she gets energized by gathering facts and figures about the things that need to get done. "*Lucy, did you order the washing machine we discussed?*" As soon as Bayo said this, Lucy realized she had spent more time researching washing machines than just concluding based on what her and Bayo had discussed. At this moment, she caught herself and proceeded to order the washing machine based on their mutual agreement, instead of gathering more facts to share with Bayo. It took them a few years of marriage to understand their talents and how to manage them for a better union.

Aria always has questions! Most of her classmates always seem ready to present and speak without what she considers to be critical thinking about the topic. This translates into Aria seeming like she pokes holes into ideas, but she genuinely has questions and cannot understand why they don't. They soon discovered that most of her classmates lead with ***Influencing*** while she leads with ***Strategic Thinking*** with ***Analytical*** as her number 1 talent. This talent usually searches for reasons and causes while also thinking about all the factors that may affect a situation

Reflect on what you have just read and for fun, imagine Andrew and Aria working together.

Reading through this, you can clearly see both the balconies and basements of each of the talents discussed. Based on the Energizers and Drainers principle we spoke about earlier, if a situation always drains more than it energizes then you need to decide the best way to handle such a situation.

Sometimes the very thing that energizes someone can drain another. Imagine what this looks like in some of your current relationships. Then imagine what it looks like in work teams, dating relationships, marriage, families, parenting and more. It is extremely important that we are self-aware enough to not only identify but also respect our differences.

It is very important to learn how to manage your talents, maximize its positive outcomes while managing its basements.

As seen above, the process of developing and deploying your SuperPowers can be a series of twists and turns, trials and errors that reveal what expressions of your abilities are most natural to you, and which ones are forced. The gap between developing your SuperPowers and dominating your world is covered by consistent progress. Ask Steve Harvey who evolved from being a standup comedian to being a popular television host. Ask Chimamanda who dropped writing poetry to focus majorly on writing short stories and novels.

The process of transforming your talents into dominance is much similar to the 300ft Chinese staircase: it's a long trek where one step leads to another. Dominating your world – using your talent in the expressions that come most natural to you until you are well known for it – is a long process where surmounting one obstacle may present a new one. It emanates from the many hours invested in applying your talents, acquiring the skills and knowledge that build your muscle in this area, and using the many opportunities accessible to you. Many of the people now ruling their world didn't start out with an intent to be popular. If your motive for expressing your talent in a particular way is to be famous or for personal gain alone, then you may not maximize your SuperPowers.

The process of deploying your talents to dominate is focused on helping you use your talents for ***impact***, and not to please. Maximizing your talents while driving impact in the process is life-changing, both for you and your recipients. People-pleasing erodes the sense of self-security and boosted self-esteem that comes with knowing that you possess valuable talents the world needs. It's counter-effective to true purpose. So, don't begin your journey to dominating your world by seeking the niche that gives the most approval or the highest pay or fame. Simply take advantage of the opportunities for expression that come your way, and then locate your niche from there.

Taking up diverse opportunities to exercise your talents also equips you with skills from the other expressions you detest, which can be applied to the ones you enjoy. Like a large sieve, such expressions will fall away over time. The result will be that you have successfully narrowed your focus to those you enjoy the most, carving a niche for yourself. This is similar to the Oprah story in the opening chapter of this book; she continued to uncover her SuperPowers and harness her strengths, which in turn transformed her entire career from a newscaster to a celebrated talk show host and a global icon.

In conclusion, dominating your world can take decades. There's no arrival point, you will continue to surmount one milestone after another as you grow on your path. As you continue on your journey, there is also the need to constantly define and redefine what your meaning of dominating your world is.

Does it mean public recognition and awards? The number of direct mentorships? Bestseller platforms for your books or leadership platforms for reach? Successful projects or causes to influence? While these milestones can serve as motivation, they must never serve as the core motive for how you choose to utilize your talents. As discussed in the chapter where we focused on connecting your purpose to your SuperPowers, dominating your world doesn't have to wait until you've possessed leverage, gotten promoted into a certain position, or have shed certain responsibilities. Start where you are, and start with what you have.

Reflection

1. Analyse your natural leadership theme based on your talents and the blind spots in this theme as a leader looking to dominate your world through leadership. List the skills you believe you need to complement your own and bring balance to your team. Find team members/relationships who have the skills you need to help you balance your team/ relationships.

2. Examine the talents of your team members/ relationships and how you can maximize them while keeping your current and future goals in sight.

3. Determine what milestones you must achieve in order to dominate your world in your sphere (e.g., winning contests, TED Talks, thought-leadership articles, mentoring others, facilitating, using your influence more etc...)

CHAPTER SIX

Energizers and Drainers – How to Manage

"

To manage energizers and drainers, choose job roles or courses of study that are about 80% aligned with your talents.

"Where focus goes, energy flows."

— Tony Robbins.

I WAS FRESH OUT of university and working my first full time job in a technology role as a Research and Development Associate. A significant part of my role involved software testing and data entry. Although it was a worthwhile experience as I learnt a lot, I soon became dissatisfied with the routine and drudgery of it all. I found my daily activities quite draining and exhausting. In retrospect, my most exciting and energizing moments were during tea breaks and lunch with my colleagues. At the time, I had no idea my experience in that role was shaped by the interplay of my energizers and drainers determined by my personality and talents.

Our personalities work in harmony with our talents and there is no 'right' or 'wrong' personality type. Just like your talents were given to you for a purpose, your personality plays a significant role in your fulfilling purpose. One of the most famous personality assessments is the Myers-Briggs Type Indicator® (MBTI®) assessment, which poses 4 main facets of human personalities as follows:

- **Extroversion-Introversion (EI):** how you get your energy and where you prefer to focus your attention.
- **Sensing-Intuition (SN):** how you take in information about the world around you.
- **Thinking-Feeling (TF):** how you like to make decisions.
- **Judging-Perceiving (JP):** how you prefer to organize your life.

If you have ever met me or heard me speak, you might wonder how on earth I took on a role that so obviously contradicted my sources of energy. There is a whole story. As a child, my father bought me a lot of gadgets and I enjoyed disassembling and reassembling them all. I grew up in the 1980s when VCRs were used for playing videos and whenever ours stopped working, I would excitedly take it apart, figure out what was wrong, and put it back together. In addition to my fascination with the mechanics behind gadgets, I excelled in Mathematics, Technical

Drawing, and for some inexplicable reason, I could draw a fairly straight line without a ruler. I also didn't enjoy reading as a child—it was way too solitary for me. It's no wonder I always got in trouble for "making noise"—I was constantly talking, as a child. Anything that required sitting in solitude for an extended period never appealed to me.

With all these factors combined, when the time came to apply to university, I was advised to study Computer Engineering or Architecture, which were presented to me as excellent choices for people who enjoy problem-solving, like me. As a result, I applied to the School of Engineering and was accepted. When I got to university, I learned that my classes would include not only Chemistry and Further Mathematics (which I excelled at almost effortlessly), but also Physics (which I absolutely detested because it required some form of reading). I couldn't see myself taking Physics-related classes, so I approached the school's career counsellor and asked for a course that would amplify my passion for computers and didn't involve Physics. She advised me to study Computer Science, to which I thought, "Sure, why not?"

By my second year of computer science, I realized the switch may not have been such a great idea. Back then, C++ was a core programming language and sometimes I would write hundreds of lines of code and it would take a single additional comma, full stop, or character to cause an error in the code I had spent several hours on. Trying to decipher the problem and get the code to run was one task that drained me. The course was ideal for introverted problem-solvers with strong attention to detail, but not for me–I was energized by working with others, and never looked forward to any assignment that required me to work alone.

Fast forward to my first full-time job; I was testing software for a newly developed solution within the organization. I was drained yet again from all the solitude the role entailed. The best part of my day was when I was interacting with colleagues. I noticed that I got really excited for coffee breaks and lunch. Although I didn't realize it at the time, the energy I gained from the breaks and other volunteer activities I participated in over the weekend would cover me for the hours I sat alone. But how long could I live for coffee breaks and weekends? How long could I look for fulfilment outside of 'work' when I could be doing work that truly fulfilled me? While my story is unique to me, I'm confident that bits and pieces of it resonate with you.

Energizers and Drainers.

Energizers are activities that give you vitality and energy on a physical, mental, and emotional level. I'm obviously an extrovert and being around people gives me energy. Positivity, WOO, Communication, Includer, and Arranger are my top five ***CliftonStrengths***® talents. I am energized by interacting with people, spending time with them, assisting them in maximizing their talents, and so much more. Your talents come naturally to you; thus, when you engage them productively, they infuse you with life and energy. Working in a role that leverages your talents is typically energizing and invigorating, causing you to operate in a way that positions you as a superstar within your team or organization.

Drainers are the exact opposite of energizers. Activities, scenarios, concepts, etc. that drain your physical, mental, and emotional energy can be classified as drainers. For me, all those hours of solitude as a university student pursuing a Computer Science degree and later, as a research and development associate, were draining. Both responsibilities required intense concentration and persistence, which may have been ideal for a less extroverted person with Focus as one of their top five talents—certainly not me. In both instances, the cliché "it's not you, it's me" maxim applied. Neither the computer science degree nor the research and development associate role were "bad", they were just not optimal for my unique talents and personality.

Even if the things that sap our energy are necessary and worthwhile, their impact on us remains. Several students, like me, have studied/are studying courses that are unrelated to their talents. Others occupy roles that largely drain them, resulting in misery, anxiety, depression and other health-related issues. You are losing energy if you are not gaining energy from what you are doing. If you spend the majority of your day doing things that drain your energy, this will surely become a major source of your dissatisfaction. This is why you must intentionally discover who you are, your personality type, and your talents – they are the foundation for everything else.

Constantly being in a situation, role, or course that drains you will not only make you unhappy, potentially cause health issues; it will also make you question whether you have any talents at all. When, in fact, it is not because you lack talents, but because you are misplaced. Everyone has talents. The goal is to focus on who you are, and your natural predispositions, rather than who you are not by deploying your energy in areas where you are less skilled. Drainers can even cause health issues, especially if you are in situations that constantly stress and exhaust you. This is because what doesn't add life to you takes it away from you! Energizers give you energy, and using your talents boosts you without even trying. Although our talents do not tell us what to do in terms of which career to pursue or which course to pursue, they do reveal our natural tendencies and give us clues that point us in the right directions so that we can enhance our efficiency.

This is not to say that…

1. A person can and should completely avoid aspects of their daily life that do not come naturally to them. I get energized by people and many of the Strategic Thinking talents fall within my lesser talents. This does not mean I cannot think strategically, I have found that strategic thinking within a group works excellently well for me. As a child, I disliked reading and preferred to be outside with other people. As an adult, I understand the value of reading and how learning from the greatest minds enriches mine, so I read despite the fact that I used to loathe doing so. Even though being alone can be exhausting for me, I understand the value of reading and make

an effort to read on a regular basis. Similarly, it can be difficult to find a job or study a course that is completely synergistic with your talents; there are always parts that require skills that aren't in your top five.

2. Toxic environments do not contribute to energy depletion. The workplace culture or educational system in your location can contribute to this. Take for instance, a workplace culture where toxic behaviours are enabled. Or one that lacks proper structure. While applying your talents consistently energizes you, increases your fulfilment, and improves your efficiency and effectiveness at work or school, the importance of a motivating and productive environment cannot be overstated.

This chapter's aim, is to assist you in identifying and focusing on what energizes you; to make you more aware of what isn't really worth your energy while learning to navigate the necessary areas that drain you.

Energizing tasks are the ones you look forward to because they are the natural application of your talents. For instance, your natural tendency to pick up on the emotions of others; compete; analyse; enjoy puzzles; spend hours alone brainstorming or researching; to make others laugh; to recognize the uniqueness in others; etc., these natural tendencies are your energizers, and engaging in them will have you brimming with vitality! Sometimes, the hours you spend engaging in activities like these feel like mere minutes.

Draining activities are outside the scope of your natural abilities, and thus necessitate more energy and intentionality to complete. As a result, drainers rarely get easier. They are the tasks you dread and put off until later, the ones that trigger your anxiety and make you feel inadequate. Sometimes, exhausting tasks are an essential component of our entire job description or course of study, and thus cannot be outsourced. You may also find yourself in a draining situation from which you cannot easily escape, such as having the key role in a negotiation committed to your hands while struggling to win others over. It is your responsibility to find ways to manage this – either by finding people within your team who may be better suited to those parts or by doing some of the tasks that energize you before facing the ones that drain you. The point is that you should not spend the majority of your work day doing what drains you. The bulk of your role should energize you, while the parts that don't should be the minority.

How to manage Energizers and Drainers.

Naturally, the talents in the 'Navigate' section of your ***CliftonStrengths*** report may not come easily and may drain you when they are an essential part of your job. Understanding our weaknesses allows us to strike a balance between the draining and energizing aspects of our jobs or studies. A weakness, according to ***Gallup***®, is anything that gets in the way of your success: behaviours that prevent people from realizing the full impact of (and return on) the expression of their strengths. According to this definition, talents in the 'Navigate' section of your strengths report may not come naturally to you, but if they prevent you from succeeding, you have a weakness that you should manage as much as possible.

How do you manage?

1. Locate the in-between.

If you get your energy from thinking and spending time alone (intellection), and you need to do things you don't like, like speaking in front of a crowd, finding an in-between would mean: spending time doing things you like, like reading a book, and then channelling that energy to an hour or two of speaking. Set a timer for an hour to do what energizes you and two hours to do what doesn't. In this way, you can redirect energy from the natural application of your talents to areas that drain you, allowing you to improve your performance in those areas.

This is especially true for those who may find themselves in situations from which they cannot get out (e.g., students who do not have the option of changing their major). Finding your in-between can also mean pursuing hobbies that excite you. While I worked at a job that drained me and looked forward to my energizers, I spent my free time volunteering in various capacities that I enjoyed. Although I approached each new week with less zeal, what I didn't realize was that the volunteer work I did infused me with the energy I used at work.

2. Recognize the purpose of the other areas.

The other things you don't like serve their own purpose, the other aspects of your job and the courses you don't like also serve a purpose, like assisting you in earning a degree. Recognizing the purpose of these other aspects of your job makes it easier to devote your energy to them. Furthermore, you will not be a student forever or remain in the same position indefinitely.

3. Collaborate — recognize what works for you.

Knowing how you assimilate as a student can help you put structures in place to get through the courses you dread. Knowing as a student that I learned better in groups was a huge help with the courses I wasn't doing well in. For our projects and assignments, I worked in groups as much as possible. The process of bringing minds together energized me and helped me pass the courses. For others, their retention is heightened when they pass on what they have read to others. This is even better as it is mutually beneficial for those who learn better in a group setting. Take tutorials or spearhead group learning sessions that are mutually beneficial to both parties. Even though your course may not be well synergized with your talents, knowing what works for you and doing it helps you get at least a passing grade in the course. Remember, the strengths-approach helps us not only recognize our own talents and natural tendencies, but also those of others, so we find the means to collaborate in mutually beneficial ways.

4. Practice something akin to the Pareto principle. In a real-life situation, whether work or study, no course or role is 100% synergized with our natural talents. There is usually that portion that we dread facing or try to delegate as much as possible because, more often than not, they lie outside the scope of our natural talents and therefore drain our energy. To manage energizers and drainers, choose job roles or courses of study that are about 80% aligned with your talents. This is much similar to the Pareto 80/20 rule, where 80% of consequences are derived from roughly 20% of causes.

The alternatives to managing these draining 20% include collaborating with others who have a natural talent in this area. You can also use the energy you have gathered from doing 80% of what you are naturally talented, to execute on the remaining 20% which don't come naturally to you.

5. **As a final resort, managing your energizers and drainers may require you to change your job or course of study to achieve balance.**

The journey can begin with volunteering or part-time jobs that help you explore your energizers and speaking with people who major in this area to understand the nitty-gritty of what you perceive as your energizer. This method of testing the waters before taking a swim is important to prevent the confusion that follows when a major career/course change is not well thought out.

In conclusion, remember that the most successful people intentionally:

- Spend most of their time in their area of strength (Pareto principle).

- Focus on developing their strengths as they manage their weaknesses.
- Know the strengths of the people around them.
- Empower the people around them to use their strengths.
- Leverage the strengths of others.

Reflection

Take a piece of paper and fold it in half lengthwise. Write 'Energizers' at the top of the paper and write 'Drainers' on the other side. Make a list of what you do daily that energizes you under the 'Energizers' column. Do the same on the 'Drainers' side. This exercise helps you clearly see how you are spending your time daily and how to manage your days more effectively.

CHAPTER SEVEN

The Judgment Bias

"

We are talented in different ways.

"There is no more efficient way to empower people than to see each person in terms of his or her strengths."

— Don Clifton.

WE TEND TO project our abilities onto people around us. For example, a person who possesses strong Analytical skills, would typically doubt the accuracy of unfounded evidence, peeling layer after layer to identify the root cause of a problem before accepting what is offered as truth. Prone to rejecting "simple truths" in favor of sound theories, they enjoy robust philosophical debates. They are also the go-to people when someone's 'wishful thinking' needs exposure to practicality. As a result of their natural disposition, people with Analytical talent themes may think others who have 'Harmony' as a talent theme are gullible since they steer clear of debates and seek common or middle ground instead. To possessors of Analytical talent themes, how could anyone easily accept a claim without analyzing possible loopholes? What's the big deal about conflict and friction that "the Harmonious" avoid them at all cost? In addressing matters, those gifted in the Analytical may use phrases like, "If I were you, I would...."; "If it were me, I would not have acted that way. Instead, I would have..." This approach is simply described as **'The Judgment Bias'** of our SuperPowers.

The judgment bias makes you assume that everyone is just like you and as such, should view life through the same lenses as you. In your view, the way you handle matters is optimal so it's difficult to comprehend any alternative approaches to handling issues. For instance, a person who leads with Relationship Building would typically take out time to build individual relationships that hold a team together. People in this talent group are usually energized by having conversations and forming deep connections with people. However, with the judgment bias, this person would wonder why on earth a manager who leads from the Executing theme dives right into rallying a team around objectives to be achieved without first getting to know members of the team and their talents. In the same vein, a person who leads from the Executing theme may have problems with someone who leads from the Strategic Thinking theme as strategic thinkers dedicate time to thinking and strategizing before acting. To the Executors, Strategic Thinkers spend more time strategizing and analysing than actually doing.

As established on our journey so far, our talents vary and are so unique to us that, according to ***Gallup***®, only 1 in 33 million people share the same order of talent themes as you do. This makes our talents and predispositions unique to us, though we may share similarities with many other people. By lumping us all together, the judgment bias contradicts the objectives of this book to recognize, celebrate, and harness our uniqueness. The judgment bias is associated with people who lack understanding of the workings of the strengths-coloured glasses[2]. Sadly, the judgment bias is pervasive and present in people across the world, irrespective of exposure and education. For instance, there are parents who insist on their children studying a university course believed to be their 'heritage' i.e., grandparents were lawyers; they, the parents, are lawyers; so, children ought to be lawyers. Although the choice of a career made on behalf of a child is usually done with pure

---

2. Chip Anderson, one of the leading researchers and practitioners of the StrengthsFinder tool created the 'strength-colored glasses' as an analogy for describing how viewing people through the lens of their strengths changes our perspective of how we see them.

motives on the parents' part and with the child's best interests at heart, conclusions like this are typically not born out of an analysis of the child's natural predispositions and identifying a career path best suited to harness them.

For a moment, think about the people who approach matters in a way you find difficult to comprehend or appreciate. The analytical person fails to understand why the harmonizer avoids friction but doesn't recognize that their talent helps the group reach a consensus, accelerating progress. The activator can't seem to understand why the futuristic hasn't started on the project they've been envisioning for "far too long", or why the ideator can't seem to stick to the plan instead of constantly reviewing the blueprint from seemingly random 'light bulb' moments.

We are talented in different ways. Our natural predispositions to handle matters differ, and in the same vein, our energizers and drainers differ. We must be mindful of comparing our capacity and approach to dealing with issues with others'. We need to recognize talents in others and find opportunities for collaboration over flat out judgement of their differences from us, keeping in mind that each talent, like a building, has ***'balconies'*** and ***'basements'***.

Balconies and basements.

All talents have balconies and basements. In this context, balconies are not necessarily the high tier from which we view the world; rather, they are the high, admirable, and positive parts of our talents. On the flip side, basements are the blind spots or downsides to our talents that we must watch out for. As wonderful as our talents may be, learning to harness the balconies is as important as navigating the basements. This is because harnessing the balconies of our talents is essential to turning our talents into strengths and when basements are not properly managed, it can lead to unproductiveness, costly friction and conflict.

Strength-coloured glasses.

Thus far, we have emphasized the need to view yourself through strength-coloured glasses—to recognize your talents and harness them into strengths. In the same way wearing glasses alters our natural vision, wearing 'strength-coloured glasses' helps us see ourselves in light of our strengths, and the possibilities available to us when we harness them.

Another benefit of seeing through strength-coloured glasses is that we start noticing the talents of others. The maxim 'love your neighbour as yourself' calls our attention to loving ourselves first, as the basis for extending the same sentiment to others. Without loving yourself or recognizing your talents, it becomes harder to recognize the talents of others and identify opportunities for meaningful collaboration. Seeing through strength-coloured glasses changes not only the way we see ourselves but also the way we see others.

Strength-coloured glasses also play a crucial role in conflict resolution, strengthening the case for this paradigm shift. In the context of relationships of any kind, strength-coloured glasses allow us unmask the villains in our stories by having a more balanced view of our offenders. Behaviours by colleagues, friends, family members, etc. that never fail to grind our nerves can be redefined as "basements" of their talents, keeping us aware of the "balconies". For example, if you typically view a person, who has a high level of discipline, as rigid, or someone with a natural tendency to command as overly domineering, strength-coloured glasses reveal their underlying strengths. Suddenly, you may be able to recognize how uniquely gifted they are, how their talents complement yours, and how best you can leverage their talents in your life. Since the judgment bias assumes that everyone is or should be like you and as such, a deviation from your norms are wrong, strengths-coloured glasses is an effective paradigm shift in relating with others.

Self-management.

Self-awareness is at the crux of this book. At this point, you may have recognized some of your unique talents and that of others. You probably feel empowered with tactics and strategies to turn your talents into strengths as well. You are also very likely gingered to unearth opportunities to collaborate with others talented in areas you are lacking in. This journey of self-discovery and self-awareness has undoubtedly set you on a path to dominate your world. However, no self-awareness is complete without self-management.

Self-management is the ability to regulate your behaviour, thoughts, and natural dispositions in the context of your environment. It also requires consciousness of how your talents are perceived by others. An analytical person who is hardly ever satisfied with the responses to an onslaught of questions may bear the indignation of their teachers or be notorious for turning a date into a full-blown job interview. In this context, their natural tendency to be deep and thorough might cause the date to be uncomfortable or be a source of embarrassment to the teacher, especially when the latter is unsure of the motives behind their persistence.

Self-management is just as important as self-awareness. Unless your values are on the line, you will need to manage your natural tendencies that may easily be misconstrued in certain contexts. As an analytical person, instead of bombarding a teacher with questions publicly, you could engage your teacher in a private meeting. This will give others the chance to also ask questions while giving you a one-on-one chance to ask all the questions you need to.

As mentioned in previous chapters, we get clues about our talents and that of others by paying attention. **This applies to children as well, and it is important we steward them in the right direction based on their natural talents.** Pay attention to what energizes your children, loved ones or those in your care - this will give you clues into their personality and talents which will help you guide them to becoming the best version of themselves. **Remember that we are all created differently for a purpose, it is important that we do not attempt to make our children, those under our care or loved ones into who WE desire them to be but into who they were CREATED to be!**

In summary, the judgment bias typically stems from not recognizing our own strengths or not extending the same recognition to others. We are not the same and that's the beauty of talents: collaboration. Within our differences lie great beauty and opportunities, so rather than judge others for being different from you, pay attention to their own uniqueness, celebrate them, and find ways to complement each other. Also, be conscious of how your talents come across to other people and try to manage the basements of your talents as much as possible.

Reflection

1. Take the ***CliftonStrengths®*** Assessment to understand what your talents are. Your report contains elaborate explanations on your talents, action plans to boost your potential, and blind spots (basements) you need to beware of.

2. Wear your ***strength-coloured glasses*** to spot the talents of people around you. From your spouse, siblings, colleagues, friends, and team leads to team members, find at least two talents per person and think of ways to collaborate with them.

Ready To Take On The World!

You can only become truly accomplished at something you love. Don't make money your goal. Instead pursue the things you love doing and then do them so well that people can't take their eyes off of you.

Maya Angelou

IT IS IMPOSSIBLE to Unleash YOUR SuperPowers without making the effort to intentionally discover YOU. Nothing empowers like knowledge, and nothing offers you a competitive edge in the world more than a firm sense of who you are. Knowing your identity, talents, and abilities provides you with confidence that you can flourish no matter where you find yourself.

Each chapter of this book has served as a guide for you on your individual path to discovering your talents and unleashing them. It is never too late to decide to begin this journey. As with all things, you have a choice. You can decide to close this book and do nothing, or you can decide to do something by taking action based on what you have read. This is your chance to Unleash your SuperPowers and begin or continue the Journey towards becoming the Best Version of yourself.

Despite what you may have believed in the past, your SuperPowers are needed in the world. Picture the world as an incomplete puzzle with irregular pieces, all our different pieces aka SuperPowers come together to complete the puzzle and make the world a better place.

Never forget that life is a journey, you have both been prebuilt and equipped to succeed on your own path. Success is in your DNA!

To your Success

What Next?

IF YOU WOULD like to take the ***CliftonStrengths***® Assessment, you can go to https://www.gallup.com/cliftonstrengths/en/252137/home.aspx

You can also contact me if you would like to understand the results and go through Strengths Coaching – me@folusogbadamosi.com or foluso@unleashmysuperpower.com

References

i. Petersen, D. (n.d.). Oprah Winfrey: *"align your personality with your purpose."* Stanford Graduate School of Business. Retrieved October 24, 2022, from https://www.gsb.stanford.edu/insights/oprah-winfrey-align-your-personality-your-purpose

ii. *Oxford English Dictionary.* (n.d.). Retrieved October 24, 2022, from https://www.oed.com:443/start;jsessionid=5522DC948B9B9CF6616EAA43B175BCEC?authRejection=true&url=%2Fview%2FEntry%2F104170%3Fresult%3D1

iii. Mara, W. (2005). *Oprah Winfrey*. Children's Press. https://www.fembio.org/english/biography.php/woman/biography/oprah-winfrey/

iv. Rath, T. (2007). *StrengthsFinder 2.0.* Gallup Press.

Notes